DO NOT REFREEZE

PHOTOGRAPHY BEHIND THE BERLIN WALL

Published to accompany the touring exhibition
Do Not Refreeze: Photography Behind the Berlin Wall,
curated and organised by Matthew Shaul,
Head of Programming and Operations, University of Hertfordshire Galleries.

12 April–17 June 2007
Cornerhouse
70 Oxford Street, Manchester M1 5NH
info@cornerhouse.org Tel: 0161 200 1500

8 November–21 December 2007
UH Galleries
Art & Design Gallery, College Lane, Hatfield AL10 9AB
m.b.shaul@herts.ac.uk Tel: 01707 285376

25 January–8 March 2008
Focal Point Gallery
Southend Central Library, Victoria Avenue, Southend-on-Sea, Essex SS2 6EX
focalpointgallery@southend.gov.uk Tel: 01702 534108

21 May–28 June 2008
Wolverhampton Art Gallery
Lichfield Street, Wolverhampton WV1 1DU
info@wolverhamptonart.org.uk Tel: 01902 552055

Project Assistant: Armin Bergmeier
Project interns: Cheryl Babajee, Nathan Gornall, Marco Verladi
Visual Arts Director, Cornerhouse: Kathy Rae Huffman
Exhibitions Organiser, Cornerhouse: Tereza Kotyk

ISBN 0-9550478-1-1 / 978-0-9550478-1-7

Published by Cornerhouse Publications
publications@cornerhouse.org

Edited by Nicola Freeman, Matthew Shaul
Translations: Armin Bergmeier, Cecile Malaspina, Matthew Shaul
Interview transcriptions: Cecile Malaspina
Catalogue design: Sara Jones, Belinda Phillpot

Printed by Tradewinds London

Cover image: Sibylle Bergemann, *Kirsten, Hoppenrade*, 1975 (detail)
Frontispiece and back cover: Maria Sewcz, from the series *Inter Esse I and II*, 1985–9

All photographs reproduced in this catalogue are silver gelatin prints.
All loans courtesy of the artists, Stiftung Moritzburg, Halle, and Museum der Bildende Künste, Leipzig.

Acknowledgements: Jeremy Akerman, Laura Bowen, Catherine Braithwaite, Chris Clarke, Paul Daniels, Lesley Farrell, Ros Findlay, Annette Hüsch, Rebecca Keating, Ingrid Klenner, Sarah Mayhew and staff at Wolverhampton Art Gallery, Sanna Moore, Charlotte Pedley, Mark Pettit, Kate Pryor, Phillip Radowitz, Martin Russell, Annette Schroeter, Jeanette Stoschek and staff at Museum der Bildende Künste, Leipzig, T. O. Immisch and staff at Stiftung Moritzburg, Halle, Victoria Walsh, Lesley Young.

CONTENTS

The development of autonomous photographic art in the German Democratic Republic (GDR) is perhaps one of the most unlikely stories to have emerged from forty years of dictatorial rule in Eastern Germany. Not widely known or understood outside the former GDR, these extraordinary images have been described as a 'missing link' in the history of post-war European photography.

The photographers' comparatively low profile is a remarkable testament to the efficiency with which East Germany's police state managed to neuter all forms of internal dissent. The unbending insistence that, although vitally important as a propaganda tool, photography was not 'art' also played its part in consigning these photographers to obscurity, in some cases for most of their adult lives. Yet it was this very isolation that allowed the group of no more than two dozen photographers to develop, and to hone a 'national' East German photographic tradition.

Do Not Refreeze has been in development for over four years and, as with all projects of this scale and ambition, there is an extensive list of organisations and individuals whose input and assistance has been invaluable. Clearly, without the intellectual and creative commitment and sheer hard work of the curator Matthew Shaul at all stages of the project, it would not have been realised. Beyond that, I would like to first acknowledge the help of the artists themselves and in particular Erasmus Schroeter whose extensive contacts gave the exhibition its initial shape and inspiration. Secondly, the project secured an incomparable boost with the decision of Kathy Rae Huffman, Visual Arts Director at Cornerhouse, Manchester, and her team to act as launch venue. Finally, I would like to recognise the help, understanding and commitment extended by the three major funders, Arts Council England, IFA (Germany's Institute for Foreign Relations), and the Arts and Humanities Research Council.

In closing, I want to acknowledge the continued commitment demonstrated by the team at the University of Hertfordshire Galleries, the senior management of the university, and colleagues in the Faculty for the Creative and Cultural Industries to long-term research projects which at inception are totally unproven, but which go on to make a substantial contribution to the landscape of British and international contemporary art.

Chris McIntyre, Director, UH Galleries

● ROSTOCK

GERMAN
FEDERAL REPUBLIC
(WEST GERMANY)

GERMAN
DEMOCRATIC REPUBLIC
(EAST GERMANY)

WEST
BERLIN

EAST
BERLIN

● MAGDEBURG

COTTBUS ●

HALLE ●

LEIPZIG ●

DRESDEN ●

In 1945, at the end of the Second World War, Germany was divided into four
zones of occupation: American, British and French in the west and Soviet in
the east, with Berlin also divided into four separate sectors (although it lay in the
heart of the Soviet occupation zone). Sharp differences of opinion between the
four powers about the future shape of German society and the direction of its
economy emerged almost immediately and culminated in the Berlin blockade
of 1948–9. The Soviet Union closed all land routes to the American, British and
French sectors of Berlin, forcing the western allies to supply the city's two
million inhabitants in the Berlin airlift which lasted 462 days.

The Soviet Union lifted its blockade in May 1949, but all hopes of a united
post-war Germany were dashed later that year when two separate German
republics were founded: the capitalist German Federal Republic in the west,
and the socialist German Democratic Republic (GDR) in the east. East Berlin,
although not officially part of the GDR, became its de facto capital city and
West Berlin, although not officially part of the German Federal Republic,
became an 'island' of West German society in the heart of the GDR.

A lack of democratic freedoms in the GDR and considerably higher living
standards in the west resulted in a flood of 'illegal' emigration. On 13 August
1961 this came to an abrupt halt with the construction of the Berlin Wall,
which cut off the principal route of East German emigration to the west and
substantially restricted travel between the two German states.

By the late 1980s the GDR was almost untouched by the reforms following
Mikhail Gorbachev's election as General Secretary of the Soviet Communist
Party. In September 1989 the Hungarian Government's decision to dismantle
the fortifications along its border with Austria unleashed a renewed flood of
East German emigration to the west and, for the first time since the early 1950s,
saw open opposition on the streets of the GDR's cities. By November 1989 the
GDR could no longer contain popular agitation for reform and agreed to lift all
restrictions on foreign travel. These reforms were a case of too little too late
and the Berlin Wall effectively collapsed on the night of 9 November 1989. In
the weeks that followed, the GDR's government agreed to allow free elections
and the two German states were formally unified in October 1990.

MATTHEW SHAUL

In the denouement of George Orwell's *1984*, the protagonist Winston Smith is told by O'Brien, his repellent and yet strangely paternalistic inquisitor, that if the Party were to decree it possible to defy gravity, the citizens of Oceania (one of three hermetic superstates controlling Orwell's dystopia) would be compelled to believe it. In the face of Smith's protestations to the contrary, O'Brien assures him that by keeping its subjects under tight surveillance, by constantly redrafting history, controlling the news media and systematically excluding foreign influence, it was possible for the Party, quite literally, to define the world, for all practical purposes.

Writing in the immediate aftermath of the Second World War, Orwell correctly predicted the vast industry that surveillance would become in Eastern Europe. East Germany, or the German Democratic Republic (GDR), whether by default or by design, made one of the most coherent attempts in modern history to turn Orwell's vision into reality. By some assessments, East Germany's formidable secret police, the Stasi, employed one informer (either official or unofficial) for every 6.5 members of the general public, to spy on their own people[1].

Yet in spite of the pervasive militarism, ideology and surveillance, the extraordinary paradox of the exhibition *Do Not Refreeze* is the diverse, exotic and irreverent culture that East Germany's photographers were able to document. These portfolios represent the most democratic and critical images produced during forty years of dictatorial rule and remarkably were often produced, exhibited, and sometimes even published, either with official sanction or at least without official interference.

The central questions that the exhibition addresses are: how did such an insightful and democratic documentary photographic tradition come into being in a state committed to socialist discipline and prepared to back this up with coercion?; how, in a state that tolerated no internal opposition and even denied that photography was art, did photography develop what was arguably the most plural visual lexicon of any of East Germany's visual arts?; and finally, what does this tell us about photography's relationship with the wider visual arts and its status as a visual arts discipline?

The GDR's socialist ideology flatly stated that there was: 'No social or political basis for opposition in socialist societies because the working class is in power'[2]. In the GDR's special case, unlike Orwell's Oceania, the exclusion of dissenting opinion was in all practical terms impossible: the majority of East German citizens enjoyed unrestricted access to western television broadcasts[3], and the culturally, economically and politically significant enclave of West Berlin occupied a large chunk of territory in the heart of the country.

By 'walling out' the west and generating the highest gross domestic product in Eastern Europe[4], the Communist regime of the Socialist Unity Party (SED)[5] was able to 'buy off' East Germans with free childcare, a job for life and living standards that approached those in the west. As the staunchest ally of the Soviet motherland these compromises combined with the military might of the Red Army to maintain East Germany's status quo for all but the last few months of its forty-year existence. What the SED regime, however, failed to grasp was that their own (initially quite idealistic) efforts to forge an alternative non-capitalist political and economic order, based on the functioning industrialised economy that had been inherited at the end of the war, required a currency and exchange of ideas that (perhaps as in modern China) would inevitably lead to the desire for democratic freedoms.

The GDR's one-dimensional commitment to the instrumental employment of art as a tool to cement revolutionary consciousness[6] was no less pernicious than the Nazis' state-driven system of aesthetics that had preceded it. This comprehensive rejection of the fertility and diversity of ideas that had been central to German philosophical thought for centuries encouraged creative thinkers of all persuasions to turn away from official culture. Withdrawing into themselves to create a *Nischengesselschaft*[7], or niche society, it was out of this that a self-sustaining independent visual culture, of which the photographers in *Do Not Refreeze* were an integral part, began to establish itself. At the same time, with a powerful western media on its doorstep, the need to disseminate positive and heroic images of socialist enterprise spawned a small but active community of freelance photographers working within the GDR's publishing sector – including the influential fashion magazine *Sibylle*, for which both Arno Fischer and Sibylle Bergemann carried out early commissions.

Established in October 1949, the GDR's new society was to be the natural inheritor of Germany's classical philosophical and humanist traditions[8]. Here, as in the rest of Europe, the urge to forge order from the chaos of war breathed new life into the documentary[9] practices that lay at the heart of humanist photography. The defining moments of humanist photography were the establishment of the Magnum agency by Henri Cartier-Bresson in 1947 and the paradigm shift in photography's status as an art form brought about by Edward Steichen's 'epochal' international touring exhibition *The Family of Man* in 1955[10].

It is a testament to the compelling power of the documentary aesthetic that, despite the intense ideological debates about the utility and purpose of art that raged throughout East Germany in the mid-1950s, a community of photographers with a value system substantially similar to the luminaries of the humanist tradition in the west began to coalesce in the GDR. The contribution of East German photography to European art history, however, was to remain undiscovered almost until the Berlin Wall collapsed in 1989.

Writing in 1988 on the occasion of the exhibition *Fotografie in der Kunst der DDR (Photography in the Art of the GDR)*[11], Karin Thomas, at the time the pre-eminent West German authority on the art of the GDR, states: 'Astonishingly, only very recently has photography begun to carve out a representative space for itself in public debate around the visual arts in the GDR, and this is even more remarkable when one considers that (historically), of all the visual arts, Marxism considered 'worker photography' (in particular John Heartfield and AIZ) to be a most effective weapon in the service of the working class'[12].

In the mid-1970s, whereas the traditionalist style of East German painting enjoyed a high market profile in West Germany, the international profile of East German photographers was almost non-existent. Officially, photography was cast in a permanent 'supporting role' in the grand narrative of Marxist art history and a cumbersome approach to photographic theory developed which frowned upon any kind of subjectivity or formalism[13].

The difficulty in constraining photography arose in reaching written definitions of what was and what was not acceptable within the framework of Stalinist aesthetics, but in 1977 the exhibition *Medium Fotografie*[14] made a first, faltering attempt to formulate a Marxist cultural history of photography. This extraordinarily late acknowledgement of the historical roots of the Marxist photographic aesthetic drew together an impressive collection of images by artists as diverse as Lyonel Feininger, John Heartfield and August Sander – as well as noteworthy contributions by *Do Not Refreeze* photographers Evelyn Richter and Arno Fischer – but slanted its approach to categorically reject the assertion that photography could be anything more than 'preparatory' to 'real' art. As Hermann Raum states in the introduction to the exhibition catalogue: 'The old argument about whether photography is a visual art form is finally at its end with this exhibition'[15].

While other GDR theorists, notably Berthold Beiler, the grandfather of East German photographic theory, had suggested there might be some room for subjectivity in photography, for Alfred Neumann, the editor of the catalogue for *Medium Fotografie*, photography's relationship to art could only ever be that of a sketch to a finished painting[16]. The result of this pervasive rejection of the subjective was that, even into the 1980s, cultural theorists ignored the increasingly significant photographic art being produced at the fringes of official culture by such artists as Gundula Schulze Eldowy and Erasmus Schroeter (both represented in *Do Not Refreeze*) and remained fixated on an agitational socialist photojournalism.

The contradiction of this rejection of the personal artistic thumbprint was that official press photography, of course, conveyed images not of life as it was lived, but as it was supposed to become. While some of the photographers included in *Do Not Refreeze* actually produced some of the most widely used 'archetypal' images to have appeared in the East German media, most GDR photojournalism conveyed an endless stream of images of inanely grinning worker brigades, ecstatic peasants and the predictable clichés of cold war confrontation[17].

Cultural commissars apparently understood the value of staging images to conform to their own ideological stipulations, but failed to take seriously the camera's scurrilous predisposition to create a truth defined by the person standing behind the viewfinder. From the 1950s onward a small group of photographers, generally working freelance and in loosely formed unofficial groupings, emerged with a profound scepticism of the collectivist value system[18] and cautiously began to present the world as they saw it rather than as it was supposed to be. As Ursula Arnold put it: 'The authorities wanted propaganda and enthusiasm – which no one except the Party functionaries believed in – so I kept my photography private and for myself, and made a commitment to telling the truth as I saw it.'[19]

Of all the photographers assembled for *Do Not Refreeze*, Arnold was the only one who, unable to support herself and her young son with her meagre earnings as a freelance photographer, all but gave up her work as a commercial photographer, freeing herself from the need to conform to socialist archetypes. Others, in particular Arno Fischer and Evelyn Richter, carved out enviable freelance careers, outwardly conforming but employing the techniques of overlay and pastiche to emphasise the isolation of the individual against the backdrop of a society that valued conformism and enthusiasm above all else. For some, these compromises led to major commissions from the East German state and a certain level of international recognition; for others, it imposed a system of self-censorship, or it all but ended any chance of a career in photography, forcing them to work exclusively in the private sphere (only to emerge after the collapse of the GDR). For Erasmus Schroeter it led to a complete ban on exhibition, direct opposition to the state and eventual exile.

Schroeter's austerely filmic photo essays exposing the decaying fabric of the GDR's cities and his portraits of the 'undesirables' who inhabited them by night, were a kind of farewell to a society from which Schroeter had already taken perceptual leave: he applied for an exit visa in 1980 [20]. Although Schroeter has accumulated an impressive curriculum vitae since moving to the west in 1985, very little has been written about his early work in the GDR. Asked about the suggestion that his view was withdrawn and cold and that his approach represented a 'detached voyeurism' [21], he has responded:

'Sometimes I caught myself looking on [my life in the GDR] as if all this were a film, even though this was my reality here, we (paradoxically, as this was supposed to be a society based on equality) lived in a petit bourgeois world all the way up to the political elite. My work was a kind of farewell to these things, because I realised instinctively that the period [in which I was living] was historically over. For me, personally, I knew quite clearly that I wouldn't stay here under these conditions and this realisation became ever clearer in the last years before I left for the west. I consciously looked for subjects that signified this departure' [22].

The vistas of Schroeter's *Stadtlandschaft – Ost (Cityscape – East)* series depict a society for which time seems to have stood still since 1945, a landscape replete with the echoes of past dynamism and the flaking paint of advertising hoardings offering the trappings of a consumer society that had not been available to GDR's citizens for forty years. Photographing either at night or in twilight, Schroeter's *Infrared* series shot in and around Leipzig between 1980 and 1985 exposed completely unacknowledged strata of socialist society – its miscreants and the fur- and pearl-clad representatives of an upwardly mobile middle class – and caused a sensation when published in the West German illustrated magazine *Stern* after his emigration.

While it could be claimed that as confrontational as Schroeter's photographs were, he nevertheless exercised some degree of self-censorship, the same could not be said of Gundula Schulze Eldowy's photo essays. If photography in the GDR was a barometer of the effectiveness with which the SED regime was able to maintain (or coerce) a degree of consent or complicity in the political process, Schulze Eldowy's photographs could be said to mark the point at which the shackles of control began to loosen.

Having affinities with Nan Goldin's *Ballad of Sexual Dependency*, Schulze Eldowy's essays, produced in the disintegrating community of Berlin-Mitte between 1979 and 1987, like Schroeter's *Infrared* series, unequivocally exploded the myth of the progressive worker's and peasant's paradise. Working serially across themes –

nudes, work, street photography, landscape – and in two remarkable essays, *Berlin in eine Hundenacht (Berlin on a Dog's Night;* below) and *Tamerlan,* a series charting the decline of an elderly woman into destitution, homelessness and ill-health, Schulze Eldowy captures the decline of socialist society with a plaintiff, startling poetry. Documenting a world whose infrastructure is close to collapse, she conveys impressions completely unfamiliar to British audiences: Germans represented as victims (rather than perpetrators) of the war, and a community still so traumatised forty years after the final Soviet assault on Berlin that the people have, as she has put it, 'lost their ability to dream'.

Gundula Schulze Eldowy *Lothar* (1982), from the series *Berlin in eine Hundenacht*

Although, as is amply evidenced in the detailed notes the Stasi accumulated on her, there was a great deal of suspicion of Schulze Eldowy and her work (among the general public as well as the authorities), the extent to which the socialist state had become an ideological behemoth unable to adjust to the increasing indifference with which its citizens viewed the socialist project is equally well evidenced. Perhaps because photography and photographers remained 'under the radar' of socialist cultural policy, not only was she able to work but also to exhibit. As she has described: 'I think that as the demise of the GDR approached, the authorities simply no longer had the strength to constrain me anymore. There was, however, always trouble whenever I showed. Often the curators were either thrown out of the country or had their options for advancement severely restricted after showing me. The Party's efforts to control me were never clear and always contradictory. When I first showed at Galerie Sophien Strasse 8 three Party functionaries showed up while we were installing. However, instead of taking the show down they said, "Your pictures are very powerful, especially the *Tamerlan* series. We hope that we don't end up in a similar situation at the end of our lives. We've received an order from the Party leadership to 'take the edge off' the show, but now we've seen it, we don't know what to do." So we went through the exhibition together and took down one nude, one dead person and one fat person. They couldn't read the iconography, the really subversive pictures stayed on the wall, and the audience, in general, understood this.

'There was no room for poetic licence in the Party's perceptions. They could only accept a very narrow and literal reading [of my work]. At that time photography was underestimated as a visual art form. Painting and sculpture, literature, poetry and theatre were very closely observed by the authorities. Photography less so, and that was simply because they didn't perceive it as art. I think my ability to work and exhibit can partly be ascribed to my refusal to be cowed, but I was also careful: I hid my negatives because it was obvious to me that they [the Stasi] would eventually try to arrest me.' [23]

The Stasi did intend to arrest her, but these plans were overtaken by the tumultuous events of the night of 9 November 1989 when the Berlin Wall was breached. More revealing perhaps is the workaday confusion that seems to have overcome this most feared organ of the East German state as they struggled to make sense of Schulze Eldowy's work, its effects, and her ability to evade the control of the cultural authorities and to continue to exhibit. Great interest was shown in her exhibition at the House of Culture in Treptow, East Berlin, in January 1985 and substantial resources were invested in a vain attempt to understand how such exhibitions could draw enormous audiences on the basis of word of mouth, without any advertising.

Convinced that Schulze Eldowy was a careerist charlatan, the Stasi were even more interested in her many foreign contacts and the possibility that some of them might be the agents of foreign intelligence services. Unable to stop her working, they concentrated their efforts on disseminating the opinion through informers and plants within the tight-knit artistic community that her work had 'nothing to do with art' [24]. A further and very effective strategy was to lampoon and discourage any serious discussion of her subject matter.

Overwhelmingly, in reading these files and in developing an understanding of the byzantine complexities of the police state, one cannot fail to come to the conclusion that by the late 1980s the GDR was a political system whose elite was fixated on a one-dimensional interpretation of an outmoded ideology and on the instrumental utility of art within this. What is truly extraordinary about Gundula Schulze Eldowy's photo essays is her embeddedness in the communities she photographed and the level of trust she commanded from her subjects. The East German state fundamentally failed to understand that human relationships, opinions and emotions, while they might outwardly conform, were not reducible to an ideological mandate.

Whether the isolation and constraint that GDR photography endured was a hindrance or, ironically, a stimulus to the development of these nine careers remains an open question but, unencumbered by the commercial imperatives that dogged freelance photographers in the west and enjoying the stimulus of regular contact with such photographers as Henri Cartier-Bresson and Robert Frank [25], Arno Fischer, Sibylle Bergemann, Evelyn Richter, and later Gundula Schulze Eldowy, were able to refine these impressions in the imposed privacy of the GDR. As Arno Fischer has put it: 'People have said we photographed the way we did because of our incestuous relationship and because we weren't allowed to travel, meaning we had to turn the camera on ourselves and our immediate environment, and yet when I was finally able to travel, on an official commission to mark the fourth anniversary of independence in Equatorial Guinea, I photographed in exactly the same way' [26].

There can be little doubt that the lack of seriousness with which photography was taken at the highest levels of government, the fact that while there was a working group there was no dedicated section for photography within the artists' union (which would have been under the direct control of a Party member), and crucially that there were no binding definitions of what was and was not acceptable in photography played their part in keeping photography 'under the radar' of the GDR's dictatorial state.

Photography undoubtedly challenged the dictatorship's ability to exclude dissenting opinion, and the dictatorship was, on the face of it, surprisingly tolerant of dissenting visions especially when codified in overlay and pastiche. The outright denial of photography's status as a visual art form, however, and the consequent absence, until the collapse of the Berlin Wall, of any serious study of these artists' work, has frozen the contribution of East German photography, as a coherent national tradition, out of its rightful place in European photographic history.

Humanist documentary photography, of which GDR photography is undeniably a part, is often associated with periods of epic ideological and political rupture [27]. Although these nine photographers are certainly the heirs of Cartier-Bresson and Robert Frank it might be more accurate to associate their work with a period of epic ideological *stasis*. Having finally retrieved them from the icebox to which history and indifference in post-unification Germany has consigned them, it is to be hoped that this groundbreaking exhibition will initiate a process of serious theoretical analysis of their work, as well as further exhibitions. Once thawed – *Do Not Refreeze*.

Matthew Shaul is Head of Programming and Operations
at the University of Hertfordshire Galleries.

KATRIN BLUM

Much of the photographic art that was produced in the GDR in the 1950s and
1960s was made in the public domain and bears a striking resemblance to the
western street photography of Henri Cartier-Bresson, Walker Evans and Robert
Frank. GDR photographers such as Ursula Arnold, Arno Fischer and Evelyn Richter
diverged from official photographic doctrines, shooting in the street and on public
transport. Drawing on their developing knowledge of the work of Robert Frank[1]
and others, and the Magnum aesthetic embodied in Edward Steichen's 1955
Family of Man[2] exhibition, they were keen to embody social commentary in
their work. And in pursuit of the documentary aesthetic they undertook formal
experimentation, not for its own sake but to emphasise their choices about
content. One of the most effective strategies they employed to reflect social
conditions and conditioning in the GDR was to focus on situations in which the
behaviour of the individual could be revealed against the backdrop of mass human
activity – as in the public transport system or political rallies and demonstrations.

THE PHOTOGRAPHER IN THE SUBWAY CARRIAGE

An important key to understanding early works by Arnold, Fischer and Richter
are Walker Evans' secret photographs taken on the New York subway in the
1930s.[3] Evans was fascinated with the anonymity of the subway carriage, a space
that was simultaneously intimate and public and in which a random cross-section
of the public came together for fleeting moments. He shot his pictures without
knowledge of his subjects' lives or histories, leaving much in the picture frame to

chance. And as the passengers were unaware of his concealed camera, the pictures were never posed.[4] This was as Evans intended: he was interested in depicting his subjects in an *unprepared* state. The spontaneity of the project served to highlight the influence of the photographer in staged portraiture.[5]

Fig.1 (right)
Ursula Arnold
S-Bahn 1966

Fig.2 (far right)
Ursula Arnold
U-Bahn 1967

In 1956 Arno Fischer began to secretly take pictures in a Berlin overground train, or S-Bahn. Sitting opposite his two subjects in *West Berlin* (1956; page 54) he seems to have held his camera on his lap and photographed the elderly man and woman in an upward perspective. There is little indication of the surrounding carriage and none whatsoever of the city of Berlin. Nevertheless, the picture appeared in *Situation Berlin*, a book initially prohibited in the GDR but belatedly published in 2001. It is one of a number of street photographs taken in West and East Berlin before the construction of the Berlin Wall, which together form an astonishing portrait of the city.[6] We may conjecture about codified political intent, or we may assume from the subjects' stout clothing and upright postures that they are well-to-do westerners, but in fact the picture gives away little about the relationship between this man and woman and whether or not they are citizens of West Berlin. Instead, one of Fischer's particular aims here seems to have been to capture spontaneous facial expressions. Perhaps like Evans, he consciously intended that his photograph should transgress the rules of traditional portraiture.[7]

In the mid-1960s, Ursula Arnold also took snapshots[8] on Berlin's subway system, developing her own distinctive style of secret portraiture.[9] *S-Bahn* (fig.1) is taken from a marked upward perspective. Again, the camera was probably resting on the photographer's lap: the bundled parcel appears to fall into the viewer's face; next to the elderly lady sits a passenger entirely hidden behind his open newspaper. The parcel and the newspaper take up an unusual amount of space within the frame. This skewed perspective, the extreme close-up, and not least, the segmentation on all sides produce an atmosphere of claustrophobia and chaos.

For financial reasons, Arnold suspended her career as a professional photographer in the late 1950s. Her increasingly experimental compositions, and the consequent likelihood of being accused of formalism or of creating images not deemed optimistic enough, made her success as a photographer in the GDR unlikely.

Fig. 3. Evelyn Richter
Strassenbahn. Dresden
(*Tram. Dresden*) 1974

Ironically, Arnold was neither interested in formal experimentation nor did she endeavour to produce an explicitly negative image of life in the GDR. Like Evans, she aimed at a realist, non-aestheticised reflection of life.

From the 1970s, Evelyn Richter took up the theme of portraits taken on public transport, and she returned to it often. While she also photographed secretly, at times she developed the motif by openly portraying groups of passengers, principally on trams. *Strassenbahn. Dresden* (*Tram. Dresden*; fig. 3) focuses on individuals lost in their own thoughts and slightly detached from their companions. In contrast to the photographs of Fischer and Arnold, a young man even meets our gaze, becoming an immediate figure of identification. The tramway is a microcosm of the GDR's 'classless society', yet appears no less individualistic than western society. Unlike GDR propaganda, the soldier is not a heroic figure but simply an individual among others. Many other photographs of this period, for example *Strassenbahn. Leipzig* (*Tram. Leipzig*; fig. 4), reflect Richter's attempt to show an unmediated and unalloyed image of GDR society, and one which appears far less optimistic and oriented towards the future than official propaganda would have stipulated.

All three photographers co-opted Evans' project to create unstaged portraits of passengers using public transport. In a society that claimed to be classless and uniform, pictures of individuals sitting indifferently in the tramway were controversial and even subversive. Such photographs were inconsistent with the obligation to 'shape the world view of the socialist person' as the influential GDR art historian Berthold Beiler demanded of photography in the 1960s.[10]

Fig. 4. Evelyn Richter
*Strassenbahn. Leipzig
(Tram. Leipzig)* 1972

ON THE PERIPHERY OF EVENTS

Richter's and Fischer's pictures of the audience on the margins of mass political
events must have seemed even more subversive to the representatives of state
power. The portrayal of a jubilant crowd was a popular subject for the GDR's
propagandist press, but to avoid any ambivalence the pictures usually provided
their own interpretation in the form of an unambiguous title. In 1959/60 the
art historian Ernst Ullmann commented on an audience picture by the press
photographer Jochen Moll (fig. 6): 'Old or young, worker or intellectual – they
are one. The photographer followed the individual and seized him before the
background of the multitude. He has extracted the face of the individual, but in
him he found the will of all, the communal will. Behind the portrayal we always feel
the like-mindedness of the people. No one is alone, all strive for the same goal'.[11]

Both Fischer and Richter approached their crowd photography very differently,
focusing on the faces of the people rather than the events they are attending.
These events, be they demonstrations, announcements or parades, take place
out of shot and are exclusively reflected in the faces of the crowd and its reactions.
Reminiscent of their subway pictures, the images capture authentic facial
expressions, the subjects not noticing the camera as they concentrate on the
event.[12] In September 1960 Fischer recorded the crowd that gathered to watch
the funeral procession for the late president of the GDR, Wilhelm Pieck (figs. 5
and 8). Unlike Walter Ulbricht, the General Secretary of the Communist Party,
Pieck was genuinely popular, and a dense phalanx of people flanked the streets

Fig. 5. Arno Fischer
East Berlin (Pieck I)
1960

of the East Berlin district of Treptow. Despite the truck laden with flowers approaching in the background (fig. 5), the viewer's gaze is drawn to something on the right, beyond the picture frame. The lack of any ostentatious grief and the detachment of the crowd recalls Robert Frank's apparently bored *City Fathers* from his 1958 book *The Americans*. The historical context is, of course, very different in Frank's work, which is obvious in the uniform dress of the city fathers, but

Fig. 6. (right)
Jochen Moll
*Jung und Alt
(Young and Old)*
1960

Fig. 7. (far right)
Evelyn Richter
*Vor der Nationalgalerie.
Berlin (In Front of
the National Gallery.
Berlin)* 1958

Fig. 8. Arno Fischer
East Berlin (Pieck II)
1960

psychologically both photographers' interest appears to be the same: they capture the empty sentiments of people participating in an official event. This lack of visible pride in citizenship was undoubtedly controversial in both Fischer's GDR and Frank's America, but while Frank enjoyed an enviable freelance career, it was impossible to publish photographs like Fischer's in the GDR press.

This was also the case for one of Richter's audience pictures, in which the clearly identifiable backdrop plays an important role. In *Vor der Nationalgalerie. Berlin (In Front of the National Gallery. Berlin;* fig. 7), dating back to 1958, Berlin's temple-like National Gallery building and the memorial sculpture of Frederick William IV on horseback tower behind a group of people witnessing an event. According to Richter, it may have been a May Day celebration in honour of 'the workers' struggle for peace and socialism', which was highly regarded by the governing elites of the GDR.[13] A woman with four children and two older women are standing among the pillars in front of the building; they follow the event with mixed interest. In a typical example of Richter's tendency toward codification and pastiche, the building and sculpture appear here as symbols of the collapsed German empire, while the obvious evidence of machine-gun damage in the two pillars framing the photograph is a reference to the unresolved political and psychological issues of the Second World War. The message is clear: with the past behind them, the spectators look towards the future. The viewer of the photograph, however, perceives another layer of meaning, not accessible to the audience of the event, in which the past and present interlock: the GDR too belongs to its own past.

Katrin Blum is a photographic historian based in Berlin.

T.O. IMMISCH

Life in the GDR ultimately would not and could not conform to the Party's ideological mandates, so it was all the more important that its presentation in the news media followed the Communists' idealistic guidelines. The GDR's news media observed – more or less strictly – the Party's dictates until the regime's sudden demise in 1989. Artists, on the other hand, were to some extent able to articulate an oppositional visual language. In particular, during the 1970s and 1980s, a clear division opened up between photojournalism and photographic art, to the extent that entire subject areas and representations of contemporary experience in the GDR from this time can only be found in the context of fine art. The development of photographic art took place in the space between the state's understanding of photography and its practical application by artists.

Although officially photography's role was to represent 'reality', or life as it was lived, and harsh criticism was reserved for staged images, in actuality press photography was systematically staged, while ideally *appearing* as a natural and immediate representation of reality. The other important demand placed on photography was that it should depict optimism for the future and the 'socialist character' of all human relationships and activities. Those who rejected this understanding of photography's role and obligations were accused of 'naturalism' on the one hand, and 'formalism' or 'subjectivism' on the other. In the 1950s such accusations could end careers, but by the 1970s, when 'broadness and variety' became the defining principles of socialist realism in the GDR, photographers were able to fruitfully exploit the new primacy of style over method.

These concepts are redolent of the more pragmatic cultural policy that attended Erich Honecker's assumption of the post of General Secretary of the Communist Party in 1971. In the 1980s, while press photography was compelled, though more gently than in the past, to adhere to the Party's ideological restrictions, fine art photography, to use Klaus Honnef's description, began to 'emancipate' itself from all attempts to control content and methodologies: rejecting the state's narrow interpretation of the medium and its applications, it started to define its own themes, representations, modes of mediation and reception.

After 1963, when the GDR closed a raft of art schools, the only remaining institution with a photography department was Leipzig's High School for Graphics and Book Art (Hochschule für Grafik und Buchkunst, or HGB, now one of Germany's pre-eminent art schools). Competition for four annual photographic studentships was fierce and the entrance examination took several days. The studies themselves prepared students for both applied and 'autonomous' photography, and graduates became members of the GDR's Association of Fine Artists (Verband Bildender Künstler, or VBK), a precondition for a freelance career.

Significantly, the majority of photojournalists were salaried, but most of the VBK photographers worked freelance, earning enough money to cover the GDR's nominal rents through architectural, advertising and theatre commissions, while allowing themselves the time and flexibility to develop their own projects. This was only possible because the cost of living in the GDR was extraordinarily low and materials were cheap. The fact that affordable childcare was also universally available allowed many women to develop high-profile careers within the GDR's photography sector.

Photojournalists were the conduit through which ideology was to be transported to the people, but the application of ideology was often fairly haphazard. A censorship practice in which chief editors arbitrarily decreed, 'Our people don't look like that' or 'That's not what our people want/need' was the norm, and the use of the possessive pronoun speaks volumes. Freelancers who were not engaged primarily in press work avoided such restrictions to a certain degree and were better placed to determine their own goals and methodologies. During the 1980s, there was a substantial rise in the number of graduates admitted to the VBK who expressed a personal, socially engaged and critical vision. The younger generation of photographers in particular had freed themselves almost entirely from stipulations on the content of their work and were increasingly able to find a public forum for it. Working thematically and serially, they began to benefit from occasional highly sought-after commissions from the Society for Photography and exhibitions in the alternative galleries that began to flourish in the mid-1980s.

Photographers' profile within the VBK had improved dramatically in 1980 when their status shifted entirely from applied artists to 'autonomous' artists with the establishment of a photography working group under the leadership of Roger Melis. This organisational change prompted growing self-confidence among artist-photographers and the development of a deeply subjective form of social documentary, an arena whose resonance was as compelling as the systematic denials of the actual circumstance of people's lives in the GDR's news media were shrill and unconvincing. Another development in the mid-1980s was the emergence of poetic staged photography. Rather than engaging directly with the often appalling social conditions in the GDR, the protagonists of this new initiative, such as Matthias Leupold, contrasted them with an imagined and subversive counter reality. To some observers this was escapism writ large, but such work played an imperative part in the reimagining of photography as a visual art form.

The contribution of a small number of institutions and individuals to the establishment of a coherent East German photographic tradition – principally Evelyn Richter and Arno Fischer, and their teaching practice at the HGB in Leipzig – should also not be underestimated. Richter and Fischer imparted an incisively subjective social documentary aesthetic, putting the entire range of their own experience and professional acquaintances in both east and west at their students' disposal. This enabled them to act as catalysts to the adoption of new and decisive influences and these were picked up by a number of state-run museums which had started collecting photography in the early 1980s: the Kupferstichkabinett der Staatlichen Kunstsammlungen in Dresden, the Staatliche Galerie Moritzburg in Halle and the Staatliche Kunstsammlungen in Cottbus.

The transformation of photography's reception and status in the GDR was also attended by the development of a range of periodicals targeted at various interest groups which wanted to publish exciting contributions by young freelance photographers. Influential publications included the entertainment magazine *Das Magazin*, the weekly journal of the culture alliance *Sonntag*, the fashion magazine *Sibylle*, the art magazine *Bildende Kunst*, the design magazine *Form und Zweck*, and *Fotografie*. While only *Fotografie* was a specialist photography magazine, all had open-minded attitudes toward 'unorthodox' photographers and photography.

Photographic projects that dealt with subject matter whose exposure was tightly controlled in the media were normally only seen in exhibitions. These included Karin Wieckhorst's images of the physically disabled in *Körperbehindert*, Renate Zeun's affecting depictions of cancer sufferers in *Betroffen – Bilder einer Krebserkrankung*, Susanne Müller's images of childbirth, and Christiane Eisler's photo essay on punk rockers, *Menschen – Leben*. The banal and grotesque aspects of everyday life were investigated: Harald Kirschner and Sibylle Bergemann documented life in the GDR's vast newly constructed housing estates; Erasmus Schroeter photographed re-enactments of the Napoleonic wars and the peculiarly German habit of adults dressing up as cowboys and Indians, causing great embarrassment to the

Helga Paris,
from the series
*Halle: Häuser
und Gesichter
(Halle: Houses
and Faces)* 1983–5

authorities; and Gundula Schulze Eldowy portrayed the old, the sick and the
poor – often naked. Some ambitious projects were carried out over several
years including Ute Mahler's *Zusammen Leben (Cohabitation)*, Christian Borchert's
and Ulrich Wüst's *Stadtbilder (City Pictures)*, while Helga Paris insinuated herself
into the life of an ancient city and its people for her series *Halle: Häuser und
Gesichter (Halle: Houses and Faces;* above). The staged photography of the 1980s
by Matthias Leupold, Thomas Florschuetz, Kurt Buchwald and Klaus Elle represents
the final chapter in a narrative in which the personal and subjective overcame
an imposed and artificial realism.

T. O. Immisch is Curator of the Photographic Collection
at Stiftung Moritzburg, Halle.

THROUGH THE LOOKING
GLASS GERHARD RICHTER'S
PHOTOGRAPHY:
INSIDE THE MISE EN ABYME

SARAH JAMES

In 1969, the German philosopher Theodor Adorno opened his last book with the line, 'It is self-evident that nothing concerning art is self-evident anymore, not its inner life, not its relation to the world, not even its right to exist.'[1] Adorno can be read as addressing the bleak situation of art after the decline of modernism and the spread of high capitalism. This was, after all, the period in which art expanded beyond its former boundaries and began to challenge established codes of representation, the collapse of which brought about the era of postmodernism. Photography, whose absorption into the category of contemporary visual art also coloured this period, is often implicated in this shift and considered to be symptomatic of the postmodern period of art production.

Adorno's comments also resonate with his infamous dictum on the impossibility of art after Auschwitz. The late 1960s heralded the final deconstruction of modernist values in all artistic fields across Europe and America; but in Germany – after the Second World War, the Holocaust, and the establishment of two republics divided by the capitalism and communism of the cold war[2] – modernism had undergone a violent annihilation. Here, artistic production perhaps had an even more fragile grip on its inner life, its relation to the world and its right to exist, than it did in the rest of Europe and America. Yet across the country, from this period onwards, photography played a central role in debates around contemporary visual art. In East Germany, in particular, the photographic medium was to play an instrumental role in the development and expansion of a new visual language.

PHOTOGRAPHY IN THE GDR/
THE GDR IN PHOTOGRAPHY

In the new German Democratic Republic (GDR), which from 1961 was cut off from the west by the Berlin Wall, the production of art was challenged by the harsh dictates of the Communist state. Socialist realism – as expounded by the Soviet Union – was inaugurated as the exclusive model of artistic production and all of the arts were understood to be operating under the direction of the political and cultural policy of the Party. Consequently, many western critics have viewed the art produced from the beginning of the East German state to its final dissolution in 1989 as entirely reducible to the dictates of a repressive and propagandistic regime.

While much of the output of GDR painters and sculptors occupied the Party political position, from the beginning of the 1970s artistic production in the GDR began to free itself from the dogmas of socialist realism. A diverse non-official artistic culture had developed, encompassing art practices that had far more in common with the conceptual, performative video and photographic work that defined the contemporaneous art worlds of the west.[3] The state's 'politics of commission' was increasingly replaced by a 'politics of purchase' (and as well as state institutions, a lively private gallery scene developed with around forty autonomous galleries exhibiting unofficial and international work)[4]. A concomitant development in photography emerged out of a diverse field of photographic practice which was increasingly difficult to contain within the state's ideologically driven doctrines on socialist art.[5]

Many East German photographers, including Evelyn Richter, Arno Fischer, Helga Paris, Erasmus Schroeter, Gundula Schulze Eldowy, Ulrich Wüst and Sibylle Bergemann, played their parts in delimiting the boundaries of this unofficial artistic world. Since photography was not considered an autonomous art by the state – and was less easy to define than the traditional art forms in terms of the demands of socialist realist aesthetics – photographers were able to explore and expand an aesthetic language that would not have been sanctioned in the more guarded domains of painting or sculpture.[6] Indeed, photography enabled the elaboration of an entirely visual discursive language that confounded the literal codes of socialist realism in its complex layering of symbolism, reference and pastiche. One photographer who was central to the evolution of this artistic photographic language and helped to shape the approach of a younger generation of GDR photographers was Evelyn Richter.

THE ART OF EXACT SEEING

After training in Dresden with the well-known art photographer Pan Walther[7], Evelyn Richter began taking photographs in the early 1950s. Always using black and white, she worked exclusively with a plate-back camera early on in her career, switching to a small-format Leica in 1968[8]. By the 1970s she had become one of the most influential photographers in the GDR.

Fig.1. Evelyn Richter
*Musikvertel Leipzig
(Music Quarter,
Leipzig)* 1976

Fig.2. Evelyn Richter
*Pförtnerin im Rathaus,
(Receptionist in the
Town Hall)* 1975

Richter's photography is coloured by a curious aesthetic and a sceptical search for pictorial veracity. Far from the lofty ideals and smiling faces of the constructed world of the East German state, real people form the central subject of her photographic enquiry. With a careful and discriminating eye, she reveals the often dreary and decrepit spaces of their lives and their interactions within them. Her images rely intently on a certain dignity and truthfulness, as an unambiguous reaction to the untruths and cultural construction of reality that dominated the visual culture of the GDR. Richter has stated: 'Whereas the avant-garde has been searching for a new visual language to expand our perceptions, I see the potential of realistic photography in increasing, with its media-specific language, tolerance and openness through knowledge and in making them [photographs], through *exact seeing*, more sensitive to each other as well as to the perception of all of life.'[9]

Her approach is almost historiographic in the way that she honours and redeems the everyday lives of East Germans: the old women who walk down Leipzig's skewed streets; the children playing on East Berlin's; the lone worker cycling across Halle's tramlines. It is as if her photographs seek to lose themselves in time so as not to become its victim, entering thus into insoluble antinomy with the necessity for objectivation. Her photography becomes an archive of the everyday. It follows the form of a kind of social investigation, and it can perhaps best be understood as operating somewhere between the photo essay of the Weimar period, the modern archives of August Sander and the conceptual series of the 1970s.

Yet Richter's work is by no means straightforward documentary photography; it also functions as a series of conceptually orientated picture cycles on certain themes, such as exhibition visitors, passengers on public transport, portraits of artists and musicians, women, and everyday life in the GDR. Further, her practice explores the medium's own distinct aesthetic: in her photography, aesthetic form becomes sedimented content, and the somatic or sensual is found in the barest documentary. Her photography distances itself from the picturesquely staged single image, as she frames her subjects thoughtfully, but awkwardly. In her famous 1976 work *Musikvertel Leipzig (Music Quarter, Leipzig;* fig. 1) the lines of buildings typically

 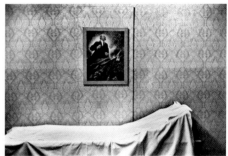

Fig. 3. Evelyn Richter
Strassenbahn (Tram)
1972

Fig. 4. Evelyn Richter
*Eingang zum
Pflegeheim
(Entrance to
the Nursing Home)*
1986

stretch off at slightly crippled angles, and a stark white winter sky hangs behind the buildings' façades. There is often a grainy quality to her prints, so that the backgrounds of her scenes become like faded newspaper reproductions. When they are exhibited, Richter's images are all framed with a fragile, rough black line around their edges – much like that which surrounds each negative on a contact sheet. This gives them a materiality that helps to disrupt sentimental aestheticism, but also removes them from straight documentary. In pursuing her photographic cycles, Richter developed a self-reflexive photography that deconstructed the artificial cultural codes of state ideology while also testing the limits of the medium.

The one constant within Stalinist aesthetics was determined by the conviction that art had to speak to the masses, so that comprehensibility and accessibility became the main criteria for socialist realist art. Formally, this was translated into a simplicity and clarity of form – a bare literalness.[10] Richter's photography consistently involves the complicated overlay and interaction of forms, which can be understood as deliberately refuting this reductive mandate. For example, she often disrupts and deconstructs the simple representation of her subjects, as in *Pförtnerin im Rathaus (Receptionist in the Town Hall;* fig. 2 and page 110) in which a woman's face is deliberately half hidden by badly placed railings, or in *Strassenbahn* (*Tram;* fig. 3), in which the passenger's image is refracted and deformed in window reflections, forming an endlessly broken portrait. In her work then, there is a definite engagement in the mechanisms bound by the photographic image itself, and in the construction of meanings that do not only reside in the details of expression or gesture that are registered by the photograph, but that become the property of the photograph itself.

RICHTER AND THE PHOTOGRAPHIC MISE EN ABYME

America and Europe in the 1970s saw the rise of conceptualism, a political and self-consciously anti-modernist art. The movement was often defined by its use of photography, so that the medium, more than any other, came to be equated with the postmodern as both a symptom and reflection of the passing of a much-maligned modern era.[11] In the work of such artists as Robert Smithson and Sherrie Levine, photography was exploited to collapse the hierarchy of object and representation, so that the copy came to be privileged above the real.[12] From this time it became de rigueur to pronounce that the photographic image had little independent meaning. The idea that the photograph was attached to the real world and underwritten by the meaning authorised by the artistic subject was therefore consciously dismantled, and the genre of documentary photography – so dependent upon the impossible reproduction of reality – was pronounced dead. Photography in the GDR did not experience the paradigm shifts ushered in by conceptualism, but as in the unofficial artistic worlds of the other states of the Eastern bloc, photographic art did play a significant part in the development of what we can call postmodern artistic strategies.[13]

Fig. 5. (right)
Evelyn Richter
*Kunstausstellung
der VBK (Art Exhibition
of the Society of
Fine Artists)* 1983

Fig. 6. (far right)
Evelyn Richter
*Ausstellung
Rudolf Hausner
(Exhibition Rudolf
Hausner)* 1979

In Richter's work, we find the exploration of photography's self-referentiality that has come to define the medium's postmodern sensibility: the mise en abyme – the 'picture within the picture' – is frequently examined, as in her iconic 1986 work *Eingang zum Pflegeheim* (*Entrance to the Nursing Home*, fig.4 and page 70) in which a socialist realist painting of Lenin is pictured hanging over an empty hospital bed, framed by kitsch 1970s wallpaper and reduced to a faded revolutionary backdrop. What was once heroic is transformed into something tragic, comic and domesticated. A past utopia is cast as having passed away. Here, Richter brings a self-awareness of the constructed nature of the image into the photograph itself, as a method of destroying the viewer's habitual response to photographs as documents that simply refer to nature.

This strategy became Richter's central exploration in her series of museum pictures. Here, the complex mechanisms of representational space are deconstructed as Richter's real photographic subjects – the gallery's visitors – are captured engaging in extraordinary interactions with the framed paintings and sculptures of the museum space. In *Ausstellung Rudolf Hausner* (*Exhibition Rudolf Hausner*; fig. 6) a young girl appears to toss a ball into the air, which fluidly falls and is fixed upon the surface of Hausner's painting of a juggling man. In another work, *Kunstausstellung der VBK* (*Art Exhibition of the Society of Fine Artists*; fig. 5), a hesitating couple seem to be nudged along by a palm extending from the abstract limbs of Hans Hendrik Grimmling's painting. In turn, their forms dissolve into his canvas. In these works the photograph's peculiar capacity to internally generate and organise meaning is brought to the fore, as Richter's camera gives form to the dialectic aesthetic relationships between forms. Representation is doubled; reality itself is literally already constituted as an image, and assumes a contingency traditionally ascribed to the photographic image.

However, Richter's interest in deconstructing and distorting the mechanisms of photographic representation did not ever descend into the infinite play of postmodern photographic art, where the reality presented by the photograph was no longer understood as the object of the image, but simply as an endless and ultimately meaningless instrument of signification. Instead, her explorations of photographic self-reflexivity remained underwritten by a fundamental commitment to the possibilities of photographic truth, autonomy, and to the idea and ethics of documentary. What makes Richter's work postmodern is that, unlike earlier modernist photography, the photographic medium is no longer regarded as transparent, nor is the photographic image presented as simply reflecting the properties of the real. In a culture so defined by the construction of false realities, it was crucial that her photography fully registered the impossibility of representing anything entirely objectively. However, the simultaneous necessity for a photographic authenticity in Richter's work and the distinctive tactility that emerges stems from a desperate desire to derive genuine experience from a photographed reality.

This commitment has remained unchanged in Richter's work, as has her photographic approach, style and aesthetic, which show a striking consistency over more than half a century. It is as if her work makes a historical stand against the endless proliferation of images that have come to define our contemporary capitalist culture. She once stated, 'In this age of total manipulation, we should try to assert the achievements of the individual author against the flood of mendacious images, works of an author who is conscious of his responsibilities, and who offers his own name as surety for their credibility.'[14] The world of total manipulation of culture defined by this past Communist state has been replaced in the present by the total manipulation of a media- and consumer-driven world. Consequently, Richter's bold decree means just as much today, if not more, than it ever did.

Sarah James is an art writer and art historian currently completing a PhD on 'East and West German Photography after 1968'.

URSULA ARNOLD

Born 1929
Studien HGB, Leipzig, 1950–5
Lives and works in Berlin

Ursula Arnold was a member of Action Fotografie, a group of young artists who were trying to free photography from the government's oppressive dictates. However, unlike her colleague Evelyn Richter (see pages 66–73), who vigorously defended her public profile, in the entire forty years of the GDR's history Arnold only exhibited a handful of her photographs publicly.

In her work, Arnold reveals life as it offered itself up to her in the streets of Leipzig and Berlin, without embellishment. The situations that she captures are ephemeral, but the photographs convey a universal mood, a feeling of disillusionment and intimate melancholia far from the government's idealised utopian vision.

Having worked as a freelance photographer for two years after her studies, Arnold became the first camerawoman on GDR television, keeping her photography career private.

U-Bahn (Underground Train) Berlin 1967

Opposite:
Berlin, S-Bahn Plänterwald (Berlin, Plänterwald Station) 1965

Berlin, 1. Mai
(Berlin, 1 May Demonstration) 1965

Opposite:
Berlin Edison Strasse 1965

Leipzig, Barfußgässchen 1956

Opposite:
Leipzig 1956

SIBYLLE BERGEMANN

Born 1941
Commercial training as a saleswoman 1958–60
Lives and works in Berlin and Margaretenhof, Brandenburg

Sibylle Bergemann commenced her photographic training in 1966 with Arno Fischer (whom she married in 1985). She worked as a freelance photographer for various magazines, including from 1970, the fashion magazine *Sibylle*. In 1990, the year of Germany's reunification, she became a co-founder of the photographers' agency OSTKREUZ and is regularly published in magazines such as *GEO* and *Stern*. In 1994 Bergemann became a member of the Academy of Arts, Berlin, where she had a comprehensive retrospective exhibition in late 2006.

Of all the contributors to *Do Not Refreeze*, Bergemann is perhaps the most journalistic, employing an 'observational' aesthetic which was commercially successful in the GDR and which has translated well into the sophisticated and wide-ranging magazine sector in the unified federal republic. She was one of the few GDR photographers to enjoy the privilege of foreign travel: with her husband Arno Fischer, she carried out a government research commission in 1984 for a proposed monument to the history of the international workers' movement. For this exhibition, Bergemann's portfolio includes images shot in locations as far afield as Paris and Los Angeles.

Seebrücke, Seelin (Pier, Seelin) 1975

Hollywood 1984

Berlin, Wiener Brücke (Berlin, Vienna Bridge) 1972

Berlin, Palast der Republik
(Berlin, Palace of the Republic) 1978

Paris, Hund (Paris, Dog) 1979

Kasan (Kazan, Soviet Union) 1973

ARNO FISCHER

Born 1927
Studied Hochschule für Angewandte Kunst,
Berlin Weissensee, 1948–51
Lives and works in Gransee, Brandenburg

After studying sculpture, Arno Fischer discovered photography almost by accident. He lived in East Berlin, but in 1953–4 he studied at the Hochschule für Bildende Kunst in Charlottenburg, West Berlin, regularly commuting between the two sectors of Berlin. In 1954, he began to take photographs in both East and West Berlin, and it was from these works that the idea for the book *Situation Berlin* evolved.

The photographs set the two parts of Berlin against each other and give an early but vivid picture of the increasing differences between them; West Berlin was already clearly a capitalist enclave. The publication of the book was planned for the autumn of 1961, but after the construction of the Berlin Wall in August that year, it had to be removed from the publishing house's programme.

Although Fischer continued to work (he took photographs for the fashion magazine *Sibylle* and of Marlene Dietrich's concert in Moscow), he declined a career as a salaried photographer and took teaching posts, first at the academy in Weißensee and later at the HGB in Leipzig.

Müritz 1956

Opposite:
Hotelportier Leningrad
(Hotel Porter, Leningrad) 1964

West Berlin 1956

Straußberger Platz, Berlin 1959

Tag der Republik, Berlin
(Day of the Republic, Berlin) 1957

Opposite:
Fuhrunternehmer, Thüringen
(Haulage Contractor, Thuringia) 1971

HELGA
PARIS

Born 1938
Studiert Ingenieur Schule für Bekleidungs Industrie,
Berlin, 1956–60
Lives and works in Berlin

Helga Paris produced her series *Halle: Häuser und Gesichter (Halle: Houses and Faces)*, an extraordinary document of the city in south-east Germany, while her daughter was studying there between 1983 and 1985. Recalling the alleyways and courtyards of Eugène Atget's Paris, *Häuser und Gesichter* presents a once-beautiful medieval city buckling under the weight of its disintegrating infrastructure, appalling environmental pollution and the ubiquitous socialist building programmes sweeping away history and tradition.

Asked whether she thought she had been allowed to photograph the way she did because photography was overlooked as a visual art form, Paris replied: 'I experienced the underestimation in Leipzig when a West Berlin publisher put out a book of my work entitled *Women in the GDR*. Helga Schubert from the GDR wrote the text, which had to be submitted to the censor. The photographs, however, were completely ignored. This was very strange and I completely agree that in this sense photography was often underestimated. But I am not even sure if I consider myself a critical photographer. Had I really approached everything with a cutting critical lens, then I would have taken different photographs. My interest at heart was always to document the simple way in which people lived in their everyday environment.

'I also experienced overestimation of photography: when *Halle: Häuser und Gesichter* was published, there was a hysterical reaction and it was withdrawn. I think this was the first time the city's administrators realised how dangerous photography was to them. The exhibition was also withdrawn, but it wasn't forbidden everywhere. I was able to show it elsewhere in the GDR, but in Halle those who were responsible for the decay of the city felt threatened. They were rather simple characters, but highly sensitive to being criticised. The photographs showed the neglect in black and white. If it had been exhibited, some might have complained about the state of the city, but it wouldn't have had the incredible amount of attention it acheived because of the ban. It even reached the magazine *ZK*.'[1]

1 Interview with the curator, Berlin, 30 March 2006

From the series *Halle: Häuser und Gesichter*
(Halle: Houses and Faces) 1983–5

From the series *Halle: Häuser und Gesichter*
(Halle: Houses and Faces) 1983–5

1-6
Kuhgasse

From the series *Halle: Häuser und Gesichter*
(Halle: Houses and Faces) 1983–5

EVELYN RICHTER

Born 1930
Studied HGB, Leipzig, 1953–8
Lives and works in Neukirch (Saxony) and Dresden

Rooted in photojournalism and realist in character, Evelyn Richter's work is at the same time deeply poetic. Well known in West Germany, she has worked professionally since the mid-1950s, developing a definitive personal style based on her psychological observations of people's social conditions and social conditioning.

Working serially across themes such as museum visitors, passengers on public transport and artists, she was excluded from her studies in the mid-1950s because of her unorthodox approach and suffered repeated intimidation and intermittent bans on public exhibition throughout her professional career.

Richter has said: 'There is an emotional weight of sufferance [in my work]. The works were codified vehicles for real social and political issues. I am of a generation that was marked by the experience of the war, and in particular the destruction of Dresden. I notice again and again that when there is a concrete, lived experience behind a work, and the work becomes the vehicle for an emotion, it usually exudes an effect. Palpable tension has always been packed into the works, and I think, this is what distinguished our art here [in East Germany].[1]

1 Interview with the curator, Dresden, 30 March 2006

Fred Malige, Komponist (Fred Malige, Composer) Leipzig 1986

Dolores Ibárruri (Republican orator of the Spanish Civil War) Moscow 1978

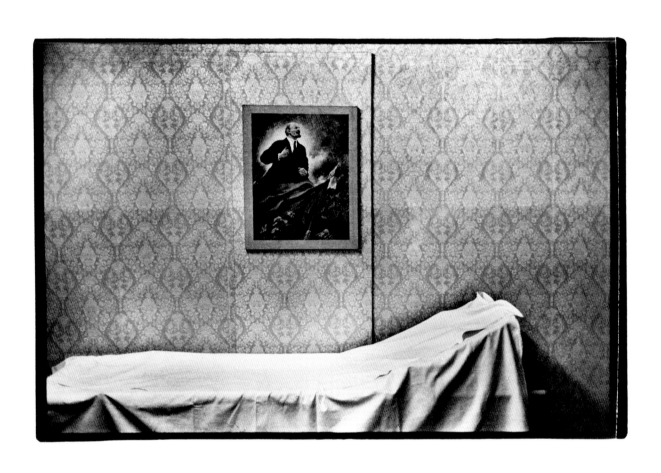

Eingang zum Pflegeheim (Entrance to the Nursing Home) Leipzig 1986

Magdeburg 1968

Pioniereisenbahner in der Strassenbahn, Dresden (Railway Pioneer in the Tram, Dresden) 1972

Kleinbahn bei Templin, Mark Brandenburg (Branch Line near Templin, Mark Brandenburg) 1970

ERASMUS SCHROETER

Born 1956
Studied HGB, Leipzig, 1977–82
Lives and works in Leipzig

Erasmus Schroeter's work has been described as having a 'scurrilous ambience imparting a profound empathy for the German psyche'[1], which is expressed through a series of generic everyman figures. He has said of his search for archetypes: 'When you photograph such an individual, an archetype who obviously conforms, but equally obviously doesn't fit into the structures of ideological state power, this is a [kind of] critique which reveals the powerlessness of the state to carry through its ideological programme.'

'I distanced myself quite consciously from the official image, which of course others did too. One difference between me and other photographers was that I always worked with flash – not only by night, when it was necessary (as, for example, in my *Infrared* series), but also during the day. The flash is what gives the pictures their staged character: it draws out a certain artificiality. This was a stylistic decision and a whole area of research that was my personal interest at the time.'[2]

1 Eugen Blume, 'Interieurs Deutscher Innerlichkeit: Gundula Schulze Eldowy', *Klopfzeichen Beglietbuch zur Doppelaustellung Wahnzimmer und Mauersprünge*, eds Eugen Blume, Hubertus Gassner, Eckhardt Gillen and Hans-Werner Schmidt, Leipzig 2002, pp. 85–7

2 Interview with the curator, Leipzig, 4 November 2006

Opposite:
*Stadtlandschaft Ost IV
(Cityscape East IV)* Altenburg 1985

*Stadtlandschaft Ost VII
(Cityscape East VII)* Magdeburg 1985

*Stadtlandschaft Ost II
(Cityscape East II)* Dresden 1985

*Stadtlandschaft Ost III
(Cityscape East III)* Leipzig 1985

Previous page:
Ein Lama soll in einen Ballsaal geführt werden
(A Llama Is Guided into a Ballroom)
Leipzig 1981

Frau mit dunkler Brille
(Woman with Dark Glasses)
Leipzig 1981

Wartende an einer Haltestelle in der Neujahrsnacht
(Waiting at a Bus Stop on New Year's Eve)
Leipzig 1981

Ein Kind Wartet (A Child Waiting) Leipzig 1981

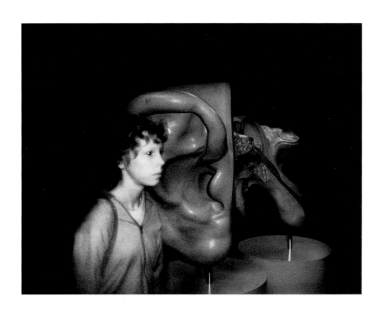

Das Ohr (The Ear)
Dresden 1981

Wartende (Waiting) Leipzig 1980

*Ein Fest Gekleidetes Paar
(A Couple in Evening Dress)*
Leipzig 1980

GUNDULA SCHULZE ELDOWY

Born 1954
Studied HGB, Leipzig, 1979–84
Lives and works in Berlin

Gundula Schulze Eldowy's serial photographic essays are characterised by an authenticity and connection with her subjects that became the central thematic spine of the diverse portfolios she created between 1978 and 1987.

One of the earliest and most noteworthy examples of her modus operandi was the series *Tamerlan* (1978–87), a photographic diary of Schulze Eldowy's relationship with a dispossessed old woman she originally met in an East Berlin park. The diary, which includes the photographer's sparklingly empathetic letters to Tamerlan and Tamerlan's replies, documents the old woman's descent into poverty, her move into a state nursing home, the subsequent collapse of her health, and her eventual death.

Tamerlan, like many of the photographer's series, underscores a desire to capture existential experience pictorially, representing an uncompromising barometer of society's preoccupations and obsessions. Making no attempt to paper over the cracks in the system, Schulze Eldowy's work pulled sharply away from the idealised vision that the socialist state had of itself and lent itself poorly to rigid ideological interference.

With her portrayals of the GDR workplace and exposure of the wretched existence of many workers, she exploded the myth of the 'heroic worker' that was so central to socialist folklore. With this approach, Schulze Eldowy, along with other young GDR photographers, began to develop an 'aesthetic of reality' that went far beyond mere criticism of the GDR's socialist system.[1]

1 Eugen Blume, 'Interieurs Deutscher Innerlichkeit: Gundula Schulze Eldowy', *Klopfzeichen Beglietbuch zur Doppelaustellung Wahnzimmer und Mauersprünge,* eds Eugen Blume, Hubertus Gassner, Eckhardt Gillen and Hans-Werner Schmidt, Leipzig 2002, pp. 81–4

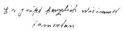
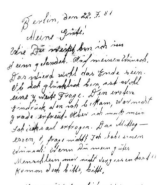

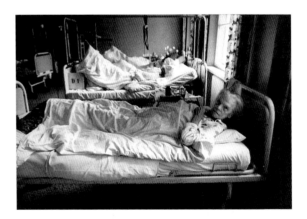
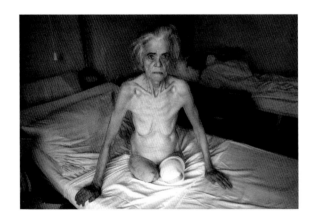

From the series *Tamerlan* 1978–1987

Top to bottom, left to right:
Kollwitz Platz, Berlin 1979
Tamerlan's Apartment, Berlin 1980
Arteriosclerotic, Berlin 1981
Hospital Dimitroff Strasse, Berlin 1981
Care Home, Berlin Blankenburg, 1981
Hospital Dimitroff Strasse, Berlin 1981
Tamerlan, Berlin 1987

From the series *Landschaften (Landscapes)*

Clockwise from top left:
Snow 1980s
Wittenberg 1980s
Poland 1980s
Saarmund 1980s
Bed 1980s
Saarmund 1980s

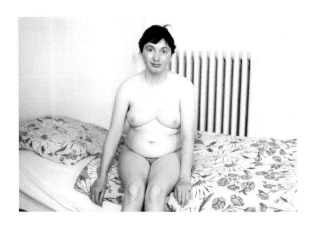

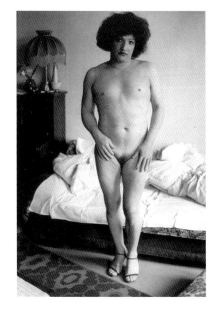

From the series *Aktporträts (Nudes)*

Clockwise from top left:
Ringo & Viola, Berlin 1983
Lothar, Berlin 1983
Gabi, Berlin 1984
Rolli, Berlin 1986
Angelika, Leipzig 1983
Petra, Erfurt 1983

From the series *Berlin in eine Hundenacht*
(Berlin on a Dog's Night)

Clockwise from top left:
Berlin 1980
Berlin 1981
Berlin 1981
Fallen Sons, Berlin 1979
Ulla & Horst, Berlin 1982
Berlin 1982

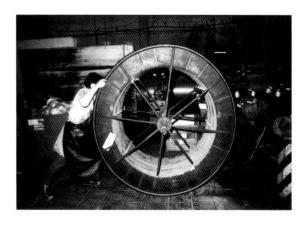

From the series *Arbeit (Work)*

Clockwise from top left:
Andreas, The Soot King 1980s
Erfurt 1987
Bad Blankenberg 1985
Erfurt 1987
Rubber Factory, Bad Blankenberg 1985
Floeha 1986

From the series *Strassen Bild (Street Photography)*

Clockwise from top left:
The Führer, Berlin 1987
Karl Marx Stadt 1980
Berlin 1982
Berlin 1982
Hoffman Kulikowski, Mielke 1984
Berlin 1980

MARIA SEWCZ

Born 1960
Studied HGB, Leipzig, 1982–7
Lives and works in Berlin

Emphasising the difficulty the GDR authorities experienced
in reaching precise definitions of what was photographically
acceptable, and pointing to the freedoms that photographers
began to enjoy in the 1980s, Maria Sewcz has said of her series
Inter Esse I and II (1985–9): 'I wanted to capture the aggression
in Berlin at this time, at being constrained, at having only a
limited range of available themes and motifs and the fact that
we only knew half of the city'. We made pictures, but we
didn't attach specific [written] meanings to them. If we had,
we would have encountered more trouble. Photos are, as it
were, an unspoken witness of the times.

'I was never really a photojournalist, always an artist or an
author, and after the early 1980s it became possible for me to
make my photography much more subjective and not to bother
with constant portrayals of workers. Ideas were encompassed
in our work but they were only suggestions – this was what
was special. At the beginning, the [photographic] engagement
[in our work] was documentary in character. But working serially
we could build a story and lay down the information in layers
very slowly, allowing our audience to read between the lines.
The multilayered approach wasn't necessary in the west, but
it's what makes our work special and is a modus operandi
specific to photography. My work has to mature and draw on
a very close knowledge of a place, person or situation. My
photography is about *engagement,* not about impressions.'[1]

1 Interview with the curator, Berlin, 3 April 2006

From the series *Inter Esse I and II,* Berlin 1985–9

From the series *Inter Esse I and II,* Berlin 1985–9

From the series *Inter Esse I and II,* Berlin 1985–9

From the series *Inter Esse I and II,* Berlin 1985–9

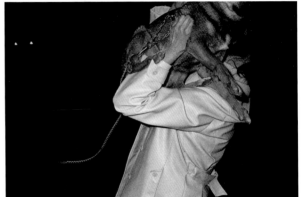

From the series *Inter Esse I and II*, Berlin 1985–9

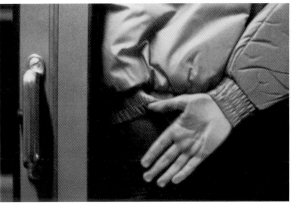

From the series *Inter Esse I and II*, Berlin 1985–9

ULRICH WÜST

Born 1949
Studied Hochschule für Architektur & Bauwesen,
Weimar, 1967–72
Lives and works in Berlin

Official reaction to Ulrich Wüst's series *Pracht der Macht*
(The Pomp of Power), shot at various locations in the Eastern
bloc and a limited number of locations in the west during
the mid-1980s, almost defines the quandary into which Party
policy on photography and its search for precise ideological
definitions had led itself.

Trained originally as a city planner in Weimar, Wüst decided
early in his career to photograph solely the built environment[1].
As he put it: 'It was impossible to get away from the idea that,
architecturally, the struggle to collectivise humanity had been a
failure. The high-rise socialist 'living units' that were constructed
to realise this were merely scenery masking city streets that had
not changed since 1945. In his photographs of the monuments
to socialist achievement which filled the cities of the Eastern
bloc, Wüst used a variety of cropping and framing techniques,
flagging up the fragile ideological foundations upon which the
socialist state was founded and the inequities these masked;
'I wanted to create a landscape of the soul, drawing attention
to what we had done to ourselves with our city planning.'

In photographing the meshing of order and disorder in the
cityscape in a state that denied that there was any disorder,
Wüst was attempting to convey to his audience new ways of
understanding their environment: 'Although [Party] functionaries
got angry about [my] photography they were unable to do much
about it. They wanted to cancel my exhibition in 1986, but didn't
because my work was clearly based in realism and they realised
they would lose the argument.'[2]

1 *Klopfzeichen Beglietbuch zur Doppelaustellung Wahnzimmer und Mauersprünge,* eds
Eugen Blume, Hubertus Gassner, Eckhardt Gillen and Hans-Werner Schmidt, Leipzig 2002, pp. 74–6

2 Interview with the curator, Berlin, 3 April 2006

Budapest 1988

Opposite:
Bust, Altes Museum, Berlin 1988

Treppe (Stairs), Nuremburg 1988

Zopf (Plait), Berlin 1988

Treptow East Berlin Soldiers 1988

Opposite:
East Berlin (Thälmann) 1988

NOTES

ONCE THAWED – DO NOT REFREEZE (pages 10–17)

1 Anna Funder, *Stasiland: Stories From Behind the Berlin Wall*, London 2003, p. 57. At the time the Berlin Wall fell, the West German media estimated the Ministerium für Staatssicherheit (the Ministry for State Security – the Stasi) had 97,000 employees and 173,000 'unofficial' informers. Comparable figures for Nazi Germany suggest that there was one Gestapo agent for every 2,000 members of the general populace, and in Stalin's Soviet Union, one KGB agent for every 5,830.

2 *Kleinen Politischen Wörterbuch der DDR, 4th edition, 1983, p. 693.* Quoted in *Informationen zur Politischen Bildung*, vol. 205, eds Horst Pötzsch and Iris Möckel, Bonn 1984, p. 33.

3 The only part of the former East Germany that experienced any difficulty at all in receiving western television broadcasts was Dresden and Eastern Saxony as far as the Polish border. This area was known in East German slang as *Tal der Ahnungslosen* or 'valley of the clueless'. For further information on the influence of West German television in the GDR, see Hans-Jörg Stiehler and Michael Meyen, 'Ich GlotzTV: Die Audiovisuellen Medien der Bundesrepublik als kulturelle Informationsquelle für die DDR', *Klopfzeichen (Mauersprünge): Kunst und Kultur der 80er Jahre in Deutschland*, eds Bernd Linder and Rainer Eckert, Leipzig 2002.

4 Anna Funder, op. cit., p. 61.

5 Sozialistische Einheitpartei Deutschlands (SED) – the Socialist Unity or Communist Party.

6 Karl Gernot Kuehn, *Caught: The Art of Photography in the German Democratic Republic*, Berkeley, California 1997, p. 10.

7 'This phrase was originally coined by Günther Gaus, the senior West German cultural representative at the West German government's "embassy" in East Berlin.' Arno Fischer, interview with the author, Gransee, Mark Brandenburg, 13 January 2007.

8 Ibid.

9 A documentary photographic style may be defined as a 'fundamentally observational and realist mode employing unmanipulated negatives and without any declared intention to change the world'. Mark Sladen and Kate Bush (eds), *In the Face of History: European Photographers in the 20th Century*, exhibition catalogue, Barbican Art Gallery, London 2006, p. 11.

10 Ibid., p. 12.

11 Halle des Historichen Rathauses der Stadt, Cologne, 20 September–18 October 1988.

12 Karin Thomas, '40 Jahre Kunstfotografie in der DDR, zwischen Sozialistischem Realismus und Realität im Sozialismus' in *Niemandsland*, vol. 7, ed. Eckhardt Gillen, Berlin 1988, p. 7.

13 Ibid., pp. 31–42.

14 Galerie Roter Turm, Halle (Saale), 4 December 1977–26 March 1978.

15 Hermann Raum, 'Medium Fotografie und Kunstwissenschaft, von eine Austellung angeregte Gedanken eines Kunsthistorikers' in *Medium Fotografie*, eds Hünecke, Ihrke, Neumann and Wallenberg, exhibition catalogue, Leipzig 1978, p. 12.

16 Alfred Neumann, ibid., p. 7.

17 'Kurt Hager, the GDR's Minister of Culture selected one image by Sibylle Bergemann of an exhausted worker enjoying a brief coffee break as the archetype of the GDR worker.' (Arno Fischer, interview with the author. Gransee, Mark Brandenburg, 13 January 2007). Peter Pachnicke, a senior East German art historian also stated: 'In predominantly staged images the ideals of the working class were presented to the people: the sweat-covered steel worker looking energetically into the future, (his) balled fist embodying a resolute understanding of the responsibilities of the future, the smiling *joie de vivre* etched into the dust-covered face of the miner, the wizened, contemplative face of the Party worker, the comforting hand of the master on the shoulder of the apprentice. Concern for the younger generation and embracing all the peoples of the world regardless of colour – less the concrete individual and more the social type, this is what imparted the idealistic and pedagogic in these staged photographs.' 'The Search for Individuality – Portraiture of the Eighties', *Bildende Kunst*, 2/1987, p. 64, quoted in Eckhardt Gillen (ed.), op. cit., p. 10. Certainly also relevant for the development of the official face of photojournalsim in the GDR is the high regard in which the photographers of the US Farm Security Administration, notably Walker Evans and Dorothea Lange, were held by Pachnicke and other senior East German theorists – a sentiment shared by Arno Fischer and Evelyn Richter.

18 Karin Thomas, op. cit., pp. 8–11.

19 Ursula Arnold, interview with the author, Berlin, 30 November 2006.

20 Although emigration was in effect illegal in the GDR, the state nonetheless became a signatory to the Helsinki human rights protocols in 1975 which, in theory at least, guaranteed the citizens of all signatory states freedom of movement.

21 Eugen Blume, op. cit., p. 87.

22 Erasmus Schroeter, interview with the author, Leipzig, 4 November 2006.

23 Gundula Schulze Eldowy, interview with the author, Berlin, 15 December 2005.

24 Gundula Schulze Eldowy Stasi files, Bundesbeauftragte für die Unterlagen des Staatsicherheits Dienstes der Ehemaligen Deutschen Demokratischen Republik, Berlin.

25 'We enjoyed the patronage of Dominique Paillarse, a "photography fanatic" and director of the French Cultural Institute in East Berlin (the only western cultural institute in the entire Eastern bloc). Through him we were regularly able to meet and exchange ideas with Henri Cartier-Bresson, Robert Frank and Josef Koudelka.' Arno Fischer interview, op. cit.

26 Ibid.

27 Sladen and Bush, op. cit, p. 11.

UNNOTICED: THE STREET PHOTOGRAPHY OF URSULA ARNOLD, ARNO FISCHER AND EVELYN RICHTER (pages 18–23)

1 Arno Fischer in particular was impressed with Robert Frank's ability to create photographs apparently without 'preliminary aesthetic calculation'. Interview with photographers of the Direkt Group, *Bildende Kunst*, vol. 4, Berlin 1984, pp. 157–161.

2 *The Family of Man* curated by Edward Steichen and organised by the International Council of the Museum of Modern Art, New York, toured to 44 cities. The exhibition attempted to convey the universal and supranational rhythms of human society in a survey comprising 503 photographs by the leading photographers of the day.

3 Evans: 'The choice of the subway as locale for these pictures was arrived at not simply because of any particular atmosphere or background having to do with the subway in itself – but because that is where the people of the city range themselves at all hours under the most constant conditions for the work in mind. The work does not care to be "Life in the Subway" and obviously does not "cover" that subject. These people are everybody.' Sarah Greenough, *Walker Evans: Subways and Streets*, Washington 1991, p. 126.

4 Walker Evans wore his small camera hidden under his jacket and the shutter release was activated by a cable running in through his sleeve. The twilight required a long exposure and a wide aperture setting.

5 The first publications of Evans' subway series appeared in the March issue of *Harper's Bazaar* in 1962, pp. 120–5, entitled 'Walker Evans: The Unposed Portrait'. In a book format his subway photographs first appeared in 1966 as *Many Are Called*, exhibition catalogue, The Museum of Modern Art, New York. The biblical title refers back to an essay written by James Agee as early as 1940.

6 The publication intended for 1961 and already entitled *Situation Berlin* was prohibited by the GDR censor after the construction of the Berlin Wall on 13 August 1961.

7 This upward perspective resulted from the photographer's decision to work unnoticed and to accept, even to embrace, the consequences of formal mistakes, such as blurring or incidental picture frames as a style choice, as for instance in Robert Frank's photography.

8 The snapshot can be seen as a necessary technique of international street photography. It is only with the spontaneous photograph, together with its equally important selection process, that this tendency could develop.

9 These photographs were not produced for publication as Arnold gave up her ambition to work as a photojournalist in the late 1950s.

10 Berthold Beiler, 'Action – wofür?': Some Thoughts on the Exhibition Action Fotografie at the Leipzig Handelshof 1957', *Fotografie. Zeitschrift für kulturpolitische, ästhetische und technische Probleme der Fotografie*, year 12, vol. 4, Leipzig 1958, pp. 133–6. Beiler uses this article to criticise the exhibition of the Leipzig group Action Fotografie to which both Evelyn Richter and Ursula Arnold belonged: 'Without losing sight of the required technical infrastructure or of the need for formal picture construction the aim of photography should be to find our *new* people at the onset of the socialist epoch. The emphasis should be on discovering the modes of their lives, their environment, their changing feelings and the new ethical maxim that govern their lives. The quality of this third step is the route to the most important themes of our time. *Action* alone is not enough but rather one should ask 'action – what for?', and the answer to this question should never be the technically accomplished photograph as an end in itself nor, in general, the meaning of an image in and of itself, but rather the photograph that makes a contribution to the world view of the socialist person and his place within it.'

11 Ernst Ullmann, 'Dem Neuen auf der Spur', *Fotojahrbuch 1959/60*, Halle 1959, p. 51.

12 The tradition of audience pictures dates back to the 18th century. An early example is William Hogarth's etching of *The Laughing Audience* (1733). The subject re-emerged in the 19th century with Honoré Daumier, who in 1864 produced a lithograph in a series entitled *Croquis pris au théâtre* which showed an audience in the theatre. The philistine admiration of the proceedings on stage is exemplified by six people in the foreground, acting as a *pars pro toto* of the uncritical crowd. In photography, audience pictures first appeared before the First World War in the context of press reportage, when they proved useful to record the presence of a prominent figure at an event, for example, or when a large audience could convey the importance of an event. The 1920s and early 1930s saw a flowering of audience pictures in the photographic press. In the Third Reich the audience picture became a central motif for propaganda, usually showing a massive jubilant crowd, in which all sorts of age groups were present, in order to witness the homogeneity of the *Volksgemeinschaft*, the togetherness of the people.

13 Interview with Evelyn Richter, Dresden, 24 June 2006.

EVELYN RICHTER'S PHOTOGRAPHY: INSIDE THE MISE EN ABYME
(pages 28–33)

1 Theodor W. Adorno, Aesthetic Theory, London 2002, p. 1.

2 From 1945, for nearly 45 years, Germany was divided into two separate countries – the socialist German Democratic Republic in the east and the Federal Republic of Germany in the west – each with its own currency, political system and social structure. From 1961, and for 28 years, the Berlin Wall enforced this division and stood as a symbol of the separation of Germany. On the divided post-war Germany and the cold war climate, see Mary Fulbrook, Interpretations of the Two Germanies 1945–1990, London 2000

3 See Karin Thomas, 'Art in Germany 1945–1982', Contemporary Germany: Politics and Culture, eds Charles Burdick, Hans-Adolf Jacobsen, Winfried Kudszus, Boulder and London 1984, p. 415.

4 The first private gallery was set up by Jürgen Schweinebraden in the East Berliner's apartment at Duncker Strasse 17 in 1974, in the city's liberal and artistic district of Prenzlauer Berg. Between 1974 and 1980, Schweinebraden presented around 67 exhibitions of national and international contemporary art, and without official permission hosted events with art actions and concerts, including the first video performance in the GDR. See Bernd Lindner, 'Eingeschränkte Öffentlichkeit? Die alternative Galerieszene in der DDR und ihr Publikum', *Blick zurück – im Zorn? Die Gegenwart der Vergangenheit*, ed. Jürgen Schweinebraden, Niedenstein 1998, pp. 225–33.

5 On the diversity of photographic practices in the GDR, see Andreas Krase, 'Das Authentische des Wirklichen. Künstlerische Photographie in der DDR', *Kunst in der DDR. Eine Retrospektive der Nationalgalerie*, eds Eugen Blume and Roland März, Berlin 2003, pp. 79–80.

6 On the ambiguous place of photography within the official art world of East Germany, see *Recollecting a Culture: Photography and the Evolution of a Socialist Aesthetic in East Germany*, ed. John P. Jacob, Boston 1998.

7 Pan Walther (1921–1987) worked in the art photography tradition, which included photographers such as Hugo Erfurth and Franz Fiedler. As a teacher, Walther stressed classical composition and the rules of a photographic use of light. He imparted to Richter the conviction that a photograph is not just a pure copy of something, but primarily a creative product.

8 Astrid Ihle, 'Evelyn Richter: Portrait', *Evelyn Richter: Arrested Time*, Heidelberg 2002, p. 6.

9 Andreas Krase, 'The Work of Evelyn Richter', *Out of Control: East German Photography*, Boston University project organised by John P. Jacob and Karla Sachse, Boston 1993.

10 See Leonid Heller, 'A World of Prettiness: Socialist Realism and Its Aesthetic Categories', *Socialist Realism Without Shores*, eds Thomas Lahusen and Evegny Dobrenko, Durham and London 1997, p. 55.

11 On the rise of postmodern art production and photography's role in this development, see Hal Foster, *The Return of the Real*, Cambridge, Massachusetts 2001.

12 Craig Owens, 'Photography en abyme', *Beyond Recognition: Representation, Power and Culture*, eds Scott Bryson, Barbara Kruger, Lynne Tillman and Jane Weinstock, intro. Simon Watney, Berkeley, California 1992, pp. 16–30.

13 On Soviet and other Eastern bloc photographic and conceptual art, see Diane Neumaier (ed.), *Beyond Memory: Soviet Nonconformist Photography and Photo-Related Works of Art*, New Jersey 2004.

14 Evelyn Richter, lecture given in Munich, 1988, quoted in Evelyn Richter: *Arrested Time*, op. cit., p. 5.

Theodor W. Adorno, *Aesthetic Theory* (London: Continuum Press, 2002)

Berlinische Galerie (ed.), *Arno Fischer. Situation Berlin. Fotografien/Photographs 1953–1960* (Berlin: Nicolaische Verlagsbuchhandlung, 2001)

Eugen Blume and Roland März (eds), *Kunst in der DDR. Eine Retrospektive der Nationalgalerie* (Berlin: G + H Verlag, 2003)

Edition Braus (ed.), *Evelyn Richter. Stillgehaltene Zeit* (Heidelberg: Wachter Verlag GmbH, 2002)

Kate Bush and Mark Sladen (eds), *In the Face of History: European Photographers in the 20th Century*, exhibition catalogue, Barbican Art Gallery, London 2006 (London: Black Dog Publishing, 2006)

Wolfgang Dressen, Eckhardt Gillen, Sigfried Radlach (eds), *Niemandsland Zeitschrift zwischen den Kulturen*, (Berlin: Verlag Dirk Nischen, 1988)

Anna Funder, *Stasiland: Stories From Behind the Berlin Wall* (London: Granta, 2003)

Sarah Greenough, *Walker Evans: Subways and Streets* (Washington D. C.: National Gallery of Art, 1991)

Andreas Hünecke, Gerhard Ihrke, Alfred Neumann and Ulrich Wallenburg (eds) *Medium Fotografie* (Leipzig: Fotokinoverlag, 1979)

T. O. Immisch and Klaus E. Göltz (eds), *Arno Fischer. Photgraphien* (Leipzig: Connewitzer Verlagsbuchhandlung publishers, 1997)

John P. Jacob (ed.), *Recollecting a Culture: Photography and the Evolution of a Socialist Aesthetic in East Germany* (Boston: Photographic Resource Center at Boston University, 1998)

Jörg Kowalski and Dagmar Winklhofer (eds), *Diva in Grau. Häuser und Gesichter in Halle fotografiert von Helga Paris* (Halle: Mitteldeutscher Verlag, 2006)

Karl Gernot Kuehn, *Caught: The Art of Photography in the German Democratic Republic* (Berkeley: University of California Press, 1997)

Thomas Lahusen and Evegny Dobrenko (eds), *Socialist Realism Without Shores* (Durham and London: Duke University Press, 1997)

Landeshauptstadt Mag deburg, Magdeburger Museen, Stadtplanungsamt (ed.), *Ulrich Wüst, Morgenstraße. Magdeburg 1998–2000* (Halle an der Saale: Verlag Janos Stekovics, 2001)

Bernd Linder, Rainer Eckert (eds: Mauersprünge), Eugen Blume, Huberturs Gassner, Eckhardt Gillen, Hans-Werner Schmidt (eds: Wahnzimmer), *Klopfzeichen Beglietbuch zur Doppelaustellung Wahnzimmer und Mauersprünge*, (Leipzig: Faber & Faber, 2002)

Norbert Moos, *Utopie und Wirklichkeit: Ostdeutsche Fotografie 1956–1989* (Bönen: Kettler, 2004)

Reihe Werkmonografien, *Maria Sewcz. Point Out* (Berlin: Jovis Verlag, 2004)

Franziska Schmidt and T. O. Immisch (eds), *Ursula Arnold. Belle Tristesse. Photographien* (Berlin: ex pose, 2000)

Hans-Werner Schmidt (ed.), *Evelyn Richter. Rückblicke, Konzepte, Fragmente* (Leipzig: Kerber, 2005)

Inka Schube (ed.), *Helga Paris. Fotografien/Photographs* (Berlin: Holzwarth Publications GmbH, 2004)

Renate Schubert, Franziska Schmidt and Betty Fink (eds), *Sibylle Bergemann. Photographien* (Bönnigheim: Wachter Verlag, 2006)

Stiftung Haus der Geschichte der Bundesrepublik Deutschland (ed.), *Foto Anschlag. Vier Generationen ostdeutscher Fotografen* (Leipzig: E. A. Seemann Verlag, 2001)